The Salt-Wind

Ka Makani Pa'akai

The Salt-Wind

Ka Makani Pa'akai

na Brandy Nālani McDougall

Kuleana 'Ōiwi Press

Wayne Kaumualii Westlake monograph series
ku'ualoha ho'omanawanui, Series Editor

About the Wayne Kaumualii Westlake Monograph Series

Wayne Kaumualii Westlake (1947–1984) was a poet, translator, scholar, artist, editor, editorialist, Hawaiian rights/sovereignty proponent and cultural agitator. From the late 1960s to his death in 1984, he broke new ground as a concrete poet, translated Taoist classical literature and Japanese haiku, interwove perspectives from his Hawaiian heritage into his writing and art, and published his poetry locally, regionally and internationally in small presses and anthologies.

Ho'oulu Hou Wayne Kaumualii Westlake consists of Cristina Bacchilega, Mei-Li Cope (Wayne's literary executor and former companion), Jennifer Dang, Monica Ghosh, Mark and Richard Hamasaki, Keiko Hatano, Dennis Kawaharada, Kapulani Langraf, Paul Lyons, H. Doug Matsuoka, Rodney Morales, Karen Ono, Gary and Merle Pak, Michael Puleloa, Cavan Scanlan, Robert Sullivan, Shinichi Takahashi, Albert Wendt, Reina Whaitiri and Holly Yamada. They, along with artists, authors, editors, publishers, Wayne's friends, colleagues and supporters helped finance the University of Hawai'i's forthcoming collection of Westlake's poetry.

Additional funds raised at the October 20, 2006 silent auction at THIRTYNINEHOTEL were donated to Kuleana 'Ōiwi Press. As a result, 'Ōiwi has established a monograph series in Westlake's name. This new book series features work by artists and authors of Hawaiian ancestry. Māhealani Perez-Wendt's *Uluhaimalama* (2007) was the first book featured in this series. Brandy Nālani McDougall's *The Salt-Wind, Ka Makani Pa'akai* (2008) is the second.

Nui koʻu mahalo no nā akua e noho mau, Haleakalā, Maui, kuʻu ʻāina hānau, nā ʻaumākua no ka malama ʻana, a kuʻu mau kūpuna mai Maui, Hawaiʻi, Oʻahu, Kauaʻi, Pākē, a me Kekokia. I am also tremendously grateful to my kūpuna, Leinaʻala Goodness Kekauoha, Clifford Nāhinu Kekauoha, Normalee Sturdevant McDougall, and Paul McDougall; my mākua, Laura Lei Uʻi Kekauoha and Jeffrey Thomas McDougall; my kaikaina, Janelle Makanani (and her kāne, Justin Shaw), Cherie Kuʻikalono, and Dawn Hālona; the Ching ʻohana (Aunty Stacy, Uncle Casey, Taylor and Keʻala); the McDougall ʻohana; the Kekauoha ʻohana; the Goodness ʻohana; Aunties Alexa and Lynn; Uncles Kaleo, David and Terrence, my ipo, Jarod Buna, and all of my friends; and last but not least, Koa, Maddie and Teddy. Mahalo nui loa no ke aloha a me ke kākoʻo.

I have also been honored to have been taught and mentored by several talented and generous kumu over the years—Albert Wendt, Haunani-Kay Trask, Cristina Bacchilega, Robert Sullivan, Garrett Hongo, Matthew Garcia, Don Bremme, Tony Barnstone, and Jim Slagel. ʻAʻohe pau ka ʻike i ka hālau hoʻokahi.

Mahalo a piha to Māhealani Perez-Wendt, Richard Hamasaki and the Wayne Westlake Hoʻoulu Hou Hui, Meleanna Aluli Meyer, Kaʻimipono Kaiwi, Malia Alohilani Rogers, Georganne Nordstrom, Alice Te Punga Somerville, Tusiata Avia, Brent Fujinaka (book design and typesetting), kuʻualoha hoʻomanawanui and the rest of Kuleana ʻŌiwi Press for making this book possible.

Contents

IV. Hāloanaka

Introduction

Tracing the lines those before me began—
their words I ask for, the old work of hands.
—"The Petroglyphs of Olowalu"

With this invocation, Brandy Nālani McDougall invites us to
accompany her on a great journey, a huakaʻi, skillfully navigat-
ing the poetic terrain of deep memory, dreams, whisperings,
fragments, family histories, spirits. Together, we explore themes
of creation and origin; colonization and loss; resistance, redemp-
tion and regeneration. Incantatory and sacred, common as salt,
nuanced and ephemeral as wind—these are the tenets of indige-
nous sensibility she summons forth in this remarkable collection
of poems, *Ka Makani Paʻakai, The Salt-Wind.*

As though carried aloft by wind itself, the poet first transports
us to a time before creation, to the time of darkness, Pō. There
we bear witness to the emergence of humankind's progenitors—
earth, sky, islands, gods—when "no one was there but the sea."

We accompany the gods Kanaloa ("turning in his sleep,
wrapped in a turbulent dream") and Kāne, as they make their
way from Kahiki Nui. Papa (Earth Mother) and Wākea (Sky
Father) bring into being Hawaiʻi, and the great gods assemble
there.

In "Memory," "The History of this Place," "Nadir" and "Back
When We Lived With Ghosts," the poet's knowledge of creation,
of gods, mediate through ancestral spirits who inhabit clouds,
grasses, leaves, branches, and even a girls' school dormitory.
"There is only the spirit of memory/that stirs the air/dark and
heavy/like a broth strained from the living," she writes.

Continuing this theme, a journal entry in "Nadir" records, "Nā
kūpuna tell me every night about how they watch the spirits
leave their bodies, yet still cling to this earth. They are all choos-
ing to stay and wrap their children in their mana like kapa moe,
rather than make the journey to Lāhaina to leap into the ocean.
They are everywhere. And still here with us. They want us to
keep living. Ola i ka ʻōhulu no nā kūpuna, no nā mamo...I heard
mama's voice today in the wind...."

In "Papatuanuku," progenitor and mother, the 'āina, itself, reminds her people:

> Remember who you came from,
> the first hā I gave you, binding you
> to me. It is my blood coursing
> through you, my 'ili stretched beneath
> you, its redness from which you
> were formed, and my voice you hear
> as your children call for you in the night

Through hardwired ancestral memory and ghost whisperings, we recall the old gods in "Huaka'i", who were commanded to

> Bring forth your fire in dance,
> your water springs and salt-swept
> waves, your huli kalo for planting,
> your sturdy, ringed trunks of niu.

In "Haumea," we stand in awe before that goddess' great handiwork, "Came stars strewn as seeds/in the heavens, spread by her hands/and sown across the dark soil of space."

As an inescapable part of Hawai'i's story, the time of colonization and its decaying effects are also recounted in "Pō," a poem of origins: "…before the cane knife's rust, the dark time of sickness,/the coming of cannons, the bitter waters drunk/before the metallic salt of blood…"

The poet in "To Takahe" asks, "Do you bury your beak in your dark green-feathered wing/to pick through the language the lice have spelled, or call/to the others, shadowing themselves under ferns?"

As if in response, a help-wanted ad for the clinical study of indigenous subjects in "Natives Wanted" includes the disclaimer, "Side effects…may include…dispossession, displacement, more disease, chronic colonization, exploitation, diabetes, alcoholism/drug abuse, severe depression, paranoia, spiritual crisis and xenophobia."

In their great unending cycle, "shadows under ferns," ancestral ghosts continue to incite deep memory and connection to the homeland Hawai'i. "[C]an you still hear/the old cries of your blood as they call you back and back?" the poet asks. In "Hō'ailona," the old cries of blood resound in dreams over many millennia, in sinewy ocean forms of eel, in sounds of rain. This is how we know our homeland, our gods, their origins.

In "Pele," a wracking violence spews forth at the goddess' birth, "blood spilled over like a river calling/I was born in red, the incendiary bloom/of the waiting sun turning in my womb,/its 'iewe spun in fire, blackened/in the heat of my throat's vibration."

The story of creation and birth take an erotic turn in "Red Hibiscus in the Sun": "Though the red flower shivers with each tickle/...her stigma hangs above her like a flare to catch/a pill of pollen in her mouth.../...opening the folds/of her thin-veined petals to/reveal the light deep in her throat."

Love as Eros is counter-posed by lechery in the stunning and heartbreakingly-rendered "Tehura," where the poet reaches across space and time to comfort and counsel, as sister, a Tahitian girl preyed upon by the syphilitic French painter and artist, Paul Gauguin. With great tenderness, the poet uses Gauguin's written account of his encounter with the young girl to indict him as oppressor, to console her as sister.

Thematically related are "Papa to Ho'ohōkūkalani" and "Kukui," the latter poem a courageous memoir of the poet's own struggle in coming to terms with a system indifferent and unresponsive to her suffering as child victim: "[S]ometimes there is no justice,/but every day, there is fire and light."

The inevitability of change, the immutable character of a people rooted in place, in Oceania—the poet also explores the juxtaposition and interplay of these great contending forces. With Hawai'i's storied history of independent sovereignhood and subsequent takeover by a America within living memory, the poet weighs in on colonization's principal impact, alienation in all its manifestations.

A young man commits suicide at Nānākuli Beach Park ("By the Blur of My Hands"); a drug-and-alcohol-addled father rifles through his wife's purse while admonishing their young daughter not to tell ("How I Learned to Write My Name"); a brooding mother ("Emma, 1993") and alienated father ("The Salt-Wind of Waiheʻe") are emotionally distant from their children; a devastating house fire delivers the coup-de-grâce ("Koa and the Burning of the Kula House") to an already broken family ("Return to the Kula House"); an impoverished single mother feeds her kids whatever the "uncles" (boyfriends) bring ("What a Young, Single Makuahine Feeds You"); a memory of the birth of a child hearkens back to happier times ("Turns of Light, the Story of Your Birth").

The indomitable character of political resistance and the possibilities it offers for personal triumph, spiritual redemption and regeneration are themes that unify "Kalena, 1945," "Kuʻulei, 1960," "Tiny Rebellions from the Kamehameha Tales," "On Cooking Captain Cook" and "Peleʻaihonua." The poet suggests that although much has been taken from Hawaiʻi's indigenous people, they will never cease in their efforts to be who they are as culture, as language, as homeland. Of their sacred patrimony, in "Lei Niho Palaoa," the poet says, "…sit proudly in your museum room/Your people will come for you soon."

Salt adds its savor throughout this collection—it pulsates in the blood, forms rivulets of tears, is spun fine by time, washes over rocks, etches glass, is sieved through valley rains—it is the commonest of elements and the poet reminds us that we are part of its vast surround. Our home is ocean, and we, too, are carried on the winds; we, too, will return, and return again.

> …The same wind will return
> to the same folds of mauna, offering over and over
> its gifts, and like nā kūpuna, always leaving, always returning.
> —"Over and Over the Return, Moʻokūʻauhau"

Māhealani Perez-Wendt
October 10, 2008

My Island Maui

There were rainbows
in this valley.
In this sky,
the sun was born.
Not a teardrop did I shed.
How I long to go back home.

Oh, where have you gone,
My Island Maui?
I have left you,
and now I miss you so.

Your valleys and your hillsides
and the ocean's roar, I know.
I'll return, yes, I will return,
My Island Maui.

We go walking
on these beaches
while the sun
is going down.
Yes, I owe my life to Maui
for the peace that I have found.

—Jeffrey Thomas McDougall, 1975

I. Pō

Pō

Before the land was tamed by industry,
the oceanside resorts and pineapple plantations,
before the cane knife's rust, the dark time of sickness,
the coming of cannons, the bitter waters drunk,
before the metallic salt of blood, the rain emptied
into rivers, the winds carved valleys and mountains,
before the earth spurted fire, birthed islands,
her churning magma and her inner core of iron,
before the stars dwarved, their coronas ignited,
before the centripetal spin of galaxies,
the unwinding gestures of time and space,
before the light and heat—

There was darkness without breath and Pō,
pressing the entirety of a universe into a shell
the size of an atomic nucleus, waiting.

Huakaʻi

ʻekahi

A greenish squall fell against
a sharp shard of the night-sky.
Who knew which way was down?
No whispers could be heard
when it all turned black—
no one was there but the sea,
Kanaloa turning in his sleep,
wrapped in a turbulent dream.

'elua

Kahiki Nui was behind them.
The great wa'a rose and sank
with every turn of the ocean,
but the stars remained, guiding
the way to the new islands
Kāne spoke of, his voice, the motion
of consumed moons hung
on the impending horizon.

'ekolu

In the beginning was the Word,
and the Word was born
to Pō, who was the dark
before the light. Kāne, it called,
then Lono, Kanaloa, Kū, Hina,
Papahānaumoku, Wākea, Haumea,
Pele, Hi'iaka: Bring forth your fire
in dance, your water springs and salt-
swept waves, your huli kalo for planting,
your sturdy, ringed trunks of niu.

Stir the darkness around you;
and bring forth the light—E ala ē!

Memory

The kūpuna are all around us now,
caressing the grasses, the leaves
on each branch—they won't let go,
just yet. Their dance makes the wind
brush the clouds across the sky—
strokes of an orangish hue
reflected in the gold of your eyes.

It is summer, a quiet breath
before the rain, and I am reminded
of how often they would say
the rain belonged to Wākea
as he reached for Papa through
the waves of air and miles of night.

But that was in the time before words—
the land, only a recent memory to the sky.

Haumea

Out of her head,
Out of her breast,
Out of her mouth,
Out of her eyes,
Out of her skin,
Out of her breath,

Came the gods who lived
off the length of her body,
offering their piko in return,

Came the soft green curve
of the sun falling into the ocean,

Came the encrusted salt pans,
the cooled fields of pāhoehoe and ʻaʻā,

Came the first young fern shoots
over the insects who work
unseen and unheard,

Came the stars strewn as seeds
in the heavens, spread by her hands
and sown across the dark soil of space,

Come the offshoots of those long germinated seeds.

Red Hibiscus in the Rain

Though the red fire-flower shivers with each tickle
of water, her stigma hangs above her like a flare to catch
a pill of pollen in her mouth, by chance. You ask her why
and listen closely, as she begins the story of her birth—
from calyx to pistil, filament to corolla—opening the folds
of her thin-veined petals to reveal the light deep in her throat.

> *He nuku, he wai ka ʻai a ka lāʻau.*
> *O ke akua ke komo, ʻaʻoe komo kanaka.*

A chant of night falls from the clouds overhead and she closes,
drawing the fire inside her petals, out of reverence for the stars.

To Takahe

Mt. Bruce National Wildlife Centre, Aotearoa

How do you answer when the wind reminds you
of oneness, when the stars ask you to tell your story,
whispering their whakapapa high above the clouds?

Do you bury your beak in your dark-green feathered wing
to pick through the language the lice have spelled, or call
to the others shadowing themselves under the ferns?

Among the loud hands that feed and breed you, that add
to the pile of brush once your nest, can you still hear
the old cries of your blood as they call you back and back?

The Petroglyphs at Olowalu

The highway to Lāhaina, newly paved
and lined in paint, curves against the mountain,

its ridges, cutting black against the gray.
Draped in dry grass, windward slopes descend

from a cloudless sky toward Olowalu,
whose pali is sharp, abrupt. Here, the waves

carve tunnels, caves. They've outlived the hands who
pressed the lines of ghosts into the cliff-face:

stiff triangular figures, broad-shouldered
men and women, the ancestors who climb

or fall against the pali wall, buffered
by ocean wind, the salt spun fine by time.

Tracing the lines those before me began—
their words I ask for, the old work of hands.

The History of This Place

Here, there are no visible remnants
    impressing the grass,
        no 'ahu
to mark the many passings

to which this place bore witness,
    housing the salt
        of tears, of bone
under the canopy of kupukupu.

There is only the spirit of memory
    that stirs the air,
        dark and heavy
like a broth strained from the living

body of *before,* saturating the earth,
    the rain sinking
        the old grief

down deep, closer to the fire within.

Pele

I was born in red, a fire call beneath
the water, lava shooting from the earth,
blood spilled over like a river calling
forth ku'u pu'u in the waiting sea.

I was born beneath, before sound, restless
for the kupukupu in its quiet
breath, falling to the black basalt in sleep,
for the tide and its lei of salted steam.

I was born in red, the incendiary bloom
of the waiting sun turning in my womb,
its 'iewe spun in fire, blackened
in the heat of my throat's vibration—

The first word was mine.
The last word is mine.

II. Kumuhonua

Kumuhonua

No one can say you don't belong here
now, though your roots are recent
as the laua'e whose blond-haired rhizome
nests upon the brown root fabric of nā palai.
Together, they cling to the porous basalt beneath,
whose fire cooled nearly 200 years ago in darkness.

Still, your name resounds in the rain
rivuleting from the roof, through the gutter.
Your blood is carried in the 'alae washed
from the cement to meet the muddy gulch.
There, your face is carved by the wind, your eyes
always fixed upon the heavens, toward salvation.

Nadir

Lawe liilii ka make a ka Hawaii, lawe nui ka make a ka haole.
*Death brought by Hawaiians takes a few; death brought by haoles
takes many.* — 'ōlelo no'eau

February 15, 1878

Mrs. Richardson knocked on the door yesterday with a pack-
age of uala, fresh poi, and a big bowl of pipi stew to make sure
that I am still eating. She has brought me food every day since
Anakala Puana's funeral last week, and I haven't had the heart
to tell her it may be all for naught in just a few short years or
months.

In her last puolo, she buried this journal under the uala. It was
wrapped in paper that was blue with flecks of white, like the
deep ocean off Kahikinui mirroring the stars. I was careful so
as not to tear it even slightly, it is so precious.

She suggested I could use this journal to record my thoughts
and practice my English. I believe that these pages will serve
me well in those regards, and also as a friend of sorts.

March 5, 1878

I spent the latter part of this afternoon among the plants. I was
surprised to find several of them still there, growing wild
among the grass. I regret neglecting them for this long. I prom-
ised Mama that I would care for them.

Even the popolo is still there in the shade of the immense
kukui tree, whose little white flowers have just started opening
like stars amid the waves of light and dark green that are its
leaves. They reminded me of the story Papa would tell about
how Mama strung them into a lei, which she wore on her head
on their wedding day, and he imagined she looked like an
anela with a thin halo of hoku.

March 19, 1878

This morning, I felt more than most days that I am the only
one left in this hale, the only one who still sees and remembers
na pua po from moeuhane. Na kupuna tell me every night
about how they watch the spirits leave their bodies, yet still
cling to this earth. They are all choosing to stay and wrap their
children in their mana like kapa moe, rather then make the
journey to Lahaina to leap into the ocean. They are every-
where. And still here with us.

They want us to keep living. Ola i ka ohulu no na kupuna, no
na mamo.

I remember this long after the sun crowns Haleakala and slash-
es its path through ka po. I hold this knowledge within me,
doubting my body's strength to carry it, even though it feeds
me through the day.

April 7, 1878

I thought I heard Mama's voice today in the wind, and I went
to visit the graves. Every single one was showered with pink
melia from the overhanging trees, making my own lei of ki and
hala seem so small in comparison. Just as I finished talking to
Mama, moani ke ala o na pua, embracing me in its folds.
Below, the valley shrouded itself in thin, low-lying clouds, and
I remembered that this moment had revealed itself to me in
moeuhane when I was just a child.

I have to keep telling myself that these days are just small parts
of this living and dying time. Small flecks of light, stars on the
ocean, to which we all must eventually return. For some rea-
son, this gives me some solace.

And now, there is purpose in writing, and an urge upwelling in me to write everything down, as if writing could slow time or even bring it back somehow. For, as na kupuna remind me—I ka olelo no ke ola, i ka olelo no ka make. In words, there is death, but there is also life.

Cane Spider

Quick, dark whir
        across the floor
                toward the unlit corner.

Long legs folded
over thorax—
        you make yourself
        small, almost gone
                in a camouflage
                        of dust.

Hairless arachnid,
born between
        the jointed stalks
                and the restless shadows
                that measure the earth—
scared, spindly thing.

They're burning our home
long into night
        and won't stop
        until morning.

By the Blur of My Hands

A standoff at Nanakuli Beach Park ended today with the loss of a
man's life. After sitting in the stolen car with a gun for six hours, the
man, identified by police as 25-year-old David Kalahiki, ran from
police toward the water where he took his own life. Kalahiki has
spent most of his 20's in prison for burglary and assault convictions.
—*The Hawai'i News Register*

The black asphalt creases the dry hillside,
sends up its heat in flares, warping the air
around me into a raw kind of fire.
And I stare at it through the cracked windshield
of this beat-up shit of a car I stole
because I knew there was no going back.
They'll find the dead man and know I killed him.
And soon, they'll find me here, their lights whirling
mad and their guns pointing back at my own.

With the ocean in the rear-view, I can't
help but cry into the wheel, hard, broken
tears for my hands, what they will never hold.
I tried, despite their useless stuttering,
their blur of deformed fingers, ugly stubs,
to make myself right, no matter. Even
drawing was too hard, colors crashed, red on
blue, over the paper and on the desk,
then the teacher's glare, whispers behind me.

I did what I could, waited twenty years
before letting my hands touch a woman
in the dark, where she wouldn't see my hands
plunge deep into her skirt, trembling as when
I washed dishes at the Red Dragon, cups
and plates breaking into shards as they fell
from my hands, like the dealer man last night,
chest open, so much blood where the bullet
tore his last breath, killed him and his money.

I cry for him now, knowing the mistakes
of my hands, that they can't blur his blood, nor
my own by this ocean, the same I fished
as a child, the cordage secure, for once,
in my grip. The waves washing salt over
rocks, the quiet glide of my hands guiding
the net in. And the pull outward after
each break, offering love more than mercy,
a faint whisper, *This is where you belong.*

How I Learned to Write My Name

It is 1981 in Kula,
and my father, cloudy and high on booze
and pakalōlō, for all his love songs
of rain and mountain mist, is unable
to stay. My mother, unable to leave
him, showers during his frantic search
through her purse for money, clattering loose
change against house keys, for any green bill
with a face. As an afterthought, he turns,
concerned now with my witness, young eyes. Hunched
over the kitchen table, I scribble
nonsense. He bribes, "I'll give you a dollar
if you don't tell." I won't. But I pretend
not to hear him, going on with the scratch,
scrawling the illegible string of loops
I insist is real writing. He doesn't
bother to yell. He has no time for it,
knows he must leave before the sound of warm
water, unsteady thumps against the tub
and her skin, stops.

                  I knew there were stories
there, staring down at the coil of *e*'s
I had just written—a bouncy ocean,
a black curly hair—that this was the start
of important work. At the paper's top,
there was my name, full, each letter composed
of dots for me to connect for homework.
My finger shadowed each sharp corner, whooshed
over straight lines and curves, almost-circles
and space—slow and careful gestures before
the pencil's touch. Then, holding the bitten
roll of yellow wood and lead, I pressed down
hard to make a mark. Sighing with each glide,
I worked, writing through the door's dull thud

behind him when he left, right through the wash
of swallowed tears behind the bathroom walls.
There was only this thrilled, measured motion:
my young hand threading dots into letters,
the fullness of my name, its shape, shouting.

Emma, 1993

I used to wake to my mother sitting
in the dark, looking out the open window
at the far harbor lights. She stared and stared,
turning the gold Hawaiian bracelets with
her name in black, wrists flashing spark after
spark. *Moani.* Straining to see her face, I wondered
what she watched for hours, heard
in night whispers from the cold Kula wind.

And though I tried to call her name, to keep
close behind, the only replies I heard
were the fading tap of her footsteps on
the porch, the metal click of her bracelets,
and the swish of her dress like a rushed gust
of wind before her bedroom door closed.

Then, I didn't know that my mother could
leave, that blood was not enough to hold her
from the kind of love that opened and closed
like a flower caught between day and night.
I watched it bloom against her face, her hands,
those men, turning and flashing, a raw fire
daughters can't give.

                    Tonight the clouds seal off
the stars, while the willful moon curves into
an open hand to offer me its muted
light. I am so quiet that the night air
whispers a love story older than blood,
of two sad halves of a flower without
symmetry, separate—the frail naupaka,
immovable—about longing that lasts
through the sharp click of metal and the flash
of hotels and miles of highways to come.

Koa and the Burning of the Kula House

When I was four, a fire overtook
   our house one night, repossessing it
with long red fingers. Our dog Koa
   survived, wriggling out of her collar,
which still clung to her chain, staked close
   to my window. We found her circling
the yard, compulsively chasing bits
   of ember still orange with heat.
They fell around her like flakes of sky,
   tiny enough to exhaust themselves
before landing. No matter. She barked
   so long at the flames that her voice
roared above the hiss and crackle
   of some unseen knick-knack breaking
open, and went from deep to hoarse
   to barely there. She wouldn't stop
until my father, broken and angry,
   threw a big rock at our roof before
it moaned and folded slowly down.
   Damn dog, it's no use, he screamed
at Koa, but she was already gone.
   She ran by me before disappearing
into the cold shadows of trees, beneath
   branches bent with heavy loads of leaves.

The Salt-Wind of Waiheʻe

In Waiheʻe the salt-wind left nothing
of your house but rusted nails, withered wood,
the howl of the ocean and the sun sinking.

For years, you kept up with the repairing,
replaced boards and glass, as you thought you should
in Waiheʻe, with its salt-wind. Nothing

could stop you from such rebuilding, nor bring
you in from outside, where you felt your blood
in the ocean's howl, in the light of the sun sinking

beneath the waves. Your daughters were watching
through a window, glass hazed by salt. We stood
out of the Waiheʻe wind and felt nothing

near love, the erosion for a windy sea
that kept you, offering only driftwood
in return. For all the ocean's howling,

we could not understand the urgency
of what stung your eyes, grayed your skin, and flooded
you with the Waiheʻe wind, leaving nothing
but our father's howl, your head slowly sinking.

What a Young, Single Makuahine Feeds You

Hamburger Helper
in every flavor,
tuna casserole,
spam casserole,
spam and corn,
spam and green beans,
spam sandwiches,
vienna sausages,
portuguese sausages,
pork and beans,
cooked corned beef,
onions and rice,
cold corned beef,
raw onions and poi,
shoyu hot dog,
sardines and onions,
canned chili,
with rice,
Spaghetti O's,
with meatballs
with rice,
McNuggets,
Cheeseburger
Happy Meals,
warm birthday cake
straight from
the microwave,
Rice Krispie treat
Easter Eggs
with your name
in frosting,
Lucky Charms,
Fruity Pebbles,
Cocoa Pebbles,
Campbell's
Tomato soup,

Chicken Noodle,
and Chicken with stars,
saimin with egg,
fried egg sandwiches,
fried bologna,
fried bananas,
fried pork chops,
fried spam,
and fried fish
or dried fish
from Uncle—
no matter
which Uncle—
you eat whatever
Uncle brings.

Turns of Light, the Story of Your Birth

for Janelle Makanani

I remember the day that you were born—
the crisp, white sun that afternoon, lighting
specks of dust caught in fragile pirouettes,
descending from the waiting room window.
Around me, grown-up legs, shifting their weight,
cast shadows on the floor. I sat alone,
watching the dance of what is barely seen,
memorizing each tiny turn of light.

In a room down the hall, our parents cried
together, as they used to do, his hand
brushing strands of hair from her face, wiping
away pearls of her sweat with a cold cloth,
very gently, as machines bleeped and flashed
to the firm beat of your heart, a small,
insistent fire stirring the dark in your chest
and her womb, whispering, *soon, very soon*—
then her breathing, then the doctors, then you.

That night, when he drove us back home, the moon,
full and white, followed our truck all the way
to Kula, casting the road in silver,
and he hummed a song he wanted to write
just for us. Smiling, she rested her head
on the glass, one arm holding you, and one
holding me. My head on her breast, my legs
stretched across his lap—it was so peaceful,
I almost fell asleep, except I knew
I had to remember for all of us.

Easter

I ask first for forgiveness—
I know my blood often turns to darkness,
crouching beast-like in the corner
to feed on meat I've bloodied
with my hands. But, I'll take the sins
of my fathers and mothers and carve
their black mark into my cheek.
I'll draw out the fire from my loins
and eyes to return it to the earth,
walk the long trail down the mountain
to feel the basalt cut into my feet—
Only grant me the strength
to look toward the waking horizon,
and gather those I love to promise
them all the light will come soon.

Dirty Laundry

My grandfather hangs our 'ohana's clothes,
cool and wet, on the line. He pauses
only to break the sticky bond between
the crumpled ones—whap! He whips them
against the air, a quick flick of both wrists
before he pins them to the cord. He knows
that one pin should hold two pieces
of clothing in its grasp—first, because it can,
and second, because there will be less
to take down when the clothes are dry.

Earlier, he emptied pockets of change,
balls of used kleenex, and old candy wrappers.
He sorted each piece by color, lights, darks,
and whites, doing each as a separate load—

while in the bathroom, at the sink,
I scrubbed the ones I didn't want him to see
with Woolite. All the dirt from the day before
runs down the drain in a dark, steady stream.
I am still the clean one. No one has to know.

Tiny Rebellions from The Kamehameha Tales

This classroom holds its windows too high
to see the ocean from my desk, by
whose feigned wood grain and carved words—lush swirls
of blue ink, gracefully drawn spirals—
I mark the minutes slowly passing.
We are a *plethora* of know-nothings,
I write, Ms. Heste is a *monolith*.
I underline each vocab word with
my red pen, spelling each carefully.
Correcting it, she'll know what I mean.

I present on Hawaiian poets,
nameless ancestors with quiet deaths,
read their words, "Kai koʻo lalo, ē.
Ua piʻi kai i uka, ē,"
as loud as I can, although I know
I am mispronouncing ka ʻōlelo.
I think Heste can sense my shame because
she rises up from her desk and says
nothing. On cue, we pull out Chaucer
to read *Canterbury Tales* in verse.
Heste announces: *And this is English.*
It is pure and unmuddled language.

Although I know she meant that for me,
I almost lose my nerve, when she reads
the knight's speech: *Gooth now youre wey; this*
is the Lordes wille. But other faces
bury their smirks in books and their pens
don't stop their note-taking. Ms. Heste bends
her gaze to mine. I act like I'm bored
yawn from a desk bolted to the floor.
Below, my carved words shout like trochees
and i mua over her *queynt myght.*

Māui

You need only to look downward
from Haleakalā to see his face
in the green folds of Puʻu Kukui,
his nose turned skyward, waiting
to be showered by the clouds.

Before him, the sun streaked through
the sky as if dying, the unmarked ʻalae
held the secret of fire, and the heavens
hung low, like damp linens stroking
the grass. After him, we had only
to assume the burden of moving
over the water between islands.

Maybe failure has always been
a part of creation—the pull of the tide
propelling us forward and the reason
for our return. It was almost in one
half-god's hands, the niu-fibered
cord drawn tight to the hook, Manaiakalani.
It was nearly in his brother's eyes,
if only they had remained fixed
on the unending, empty ocean ahead.

Yet, it will be in the grip
of his many sons and daughters
as they find their own hooks
deep in their ancestral land,
holding tight to nā ēwe of nā piko.

III. Papahānaumoku

Ma'alaea Harbor, Father's Day

My sister and I sit on rocks, watching sails and glass-
bottom boats, but you are nowhere, so we wait.
Waves glide slowly toward us, crash,
then run away, carrying the unstrung lei
we made for you this morning,
little white buds of plumeria, gardenia.
We will stare until they fade, when
we remember more of you and the sea
you loved, what you carried in your pockets:

cloudy shells, hazy beach glass. On our visits
every other weekend, you led us to the beach,
retrieved pebbles, pieces of driftwood,
lifeless angelfish, frail as ashed paper—
whatever the water had enough of, spit out.

Once, a whole bottle, salt-etched green, unbroken,
let sunlight spark a fire in your hands. Over
our young heads—a faint flash—today's sun, falling
fast into the waves, your lei still floating
toward a horizon pierced with the night's first stars.

Trumpet Heart-Song

I expect you to be here, as you always have:
your voice, a trumpet in song, your brown eyes
bluing, lit by the spark of laughter you drew
from a room, your smile, your hands building
a doll-house, fish ponds, and stained glass lamps,
the sweet smell of your pipe infusing your love—

Last night, dreaming, I wrote you a poem.
It began with quiet words, like a small boy
playing jacks alone, like a near-empty house
waiting for dawn—and grew louder, louder—
like a brass bell, a trumpet, the ocean's
roaring waves—until one couldn't hear
words, but only sounds to describe you.

I lost all of the lines when I woke
with a hard thump in my chest, and behind it
a percussion of hearts who held your hands,
laughed wide-mouthed in your arms, and cry now
to let you go, unsure if our bodies can carry
the weight of being without you, the same way
you once carried us. But then a light rain
stirs tobacco in the wind, and I can see you
in every face, hear you in every word.

Yellow Orchids

The yellow orchids about which you feigned interest
are almost all in bloom. Maybe you recall they were
just beginning to open their ripened lips to the bright
band of sun that bends its way through the curtains
in the morning. The orchids grow fuller day by day,
dawdle in the corner, polishing up each striped petal.
I know in two weeks they will begin breaking away
from the stalk, their open mouths swallowing the air-
conditioned air around them whole, before falling,
finally, to the tabletop, the carpet—I hope they hurry.

It is true that without you the days are passing slower
than usual, with every detail of every day enlarged
and stirring in its own crispness. Even so, I forget
the specifics of details of what is here when I hear
your voice—everything I had meant to share with you,
mentally collected, yellow orchids included, everything
expires, even in the wait, as the clouds outside purple
with night, and as the tradewinds persist against the glass—
Inside, the volume of my refrigerator's electric churn turns
down at the phone's sound—then your voice, its distance,
you.

Hypothetical

E Tita, you tink if we eva came home
hāpai, and we told our mākua
was cuz we wen accidentally
hiamoe in da fores' some place
and neva knew we was on da phallic rock—
You tink dey would believe?

Ku'ulei, 1960

'A'ole e 'ōlelo mai ana ke ahi ua ana ia. *Fire will never say that it has had enough.* —'ōlelo no'eau

After my mother died, I was good for another ten years. I learned to cook, and I cleaned every room from top to bottom after school. I washed and pressed my father's work clothes early in the morning, and hung them on the guava tree, so the gingered breeze could bury itself in the fabric and remind him to come home.

When he did come home, we ate together, and I pretended not to count the number of times he filled his glass of ice and bourbon before finally falling asleep on the old koa table that was a part of his inheritance.

Goodness is often mistaken for weakness, though it takes a kind of godly strength I'm thankful to have eventually lost. At 18, my father sent me to a mainland college, where I was tested in more than math and writing by accusations of copying another's assignments and comments I was meant to overhear so I could never forget the mark of my skin, nor the insignificance of my beginnings. Rather than break me, it lit a fire inside that burned in my memory.

So now, though the television and radio instruct us to *Speak American. Think American. Act American,* as the 50th state, I know better than to think that such goodness could ever be rewarded. But, like I tell my daughter, if you keep your na'au *Hawaiian,* it is easier to accept our bitter inheritance—we must *become* them to *overcome* them.

On Finding My Father's First Essay, San Joaquin Delta College, 1987

It must have been hard for him on days
when the sun hit the muddy delta,
sending up what smelled like failure,
rotten and man-made. Still, he drove
his old, rusty car down Pacific to
the college, where he sat by those
half his age who knew little of how
they would begin, how easily beginnings
turn into a thousand dark miles of water.
But they knew school, much more about it
than he did—which words to use when,
how to give nothing but the requirement,
to hide between clauses and commas.
This was his mistake of the essay
called "What Life Means to Me":

> *My shadow on the ocean's face, the frayed*
> *water behind a boat. Rainbows and valleys*
> *and leis for my daughters, that they forgive*
> *me for leaving and all that I couldn't give.*

Some nameless face read through it, asking
for predicates, circling fragments, then went on,
knowing our father's tears, yet deeming them
unremarkable. I can see his hands thumbing
the red-marked page, searching for a glimpse
of understanding and finding none, his face
burning with shame for not knowing how much
it would take to begin again, to go back across
the water. He must have left that day thinking
he had to work even harder for our love, to be
a real father, responsible and clean as grammar.

Back When We Lived With Ghosts

Kamehameha Schools, Kapiolani Nui Dormitory, 1990

We lived with nā lapu though half of that first year
before Kahu stood in the piko of our meeting circle,
and asked them politely to move on toward God.

Most were harmless, really, but kolohe—running past
our doors during study hall with heavy, unseen feet.
Remember when Lani said one blew a cold wind
on her cheek as she proved the degrees of an isosceles
triangle for homework? When the window slammed
behind Hōkū, but there was no wind? We believed
the sophomores when they saw the green lady
in the piano room. And at night we heard laughter
coming from the forest, but couldn't see anyone
among the shadows of the trees, and the furniture
shifting across the floor in the attic, where they kept
what belonged to ke ali'i Pauahi, according to Keānuenue.

But some were 'uhane—weren't they? Noelani cried
when she told us how her tūtū sat at her bed's edge
to sing her blessings of aloha before saying goodbye.

And the one I saw, and told you about—the faint outline
of a man who seemed startled by my waking from a dream.
He saw me see him, paused, then ran into the next room.
It happened quickly and I was afraid—that was my story—

But I didn't tell you how much more afraid *he* was,
standing by my bed, the same size as my father, then gone
for two years—with the same hesitance to speak.

Sisters, which ones have you kept to yourselves through the
    years?

Return to the Kula House

Night, and the road to Kula
is lit completely by the moon.
Driving, headlights off, I see shadows,
blurred pastures lined in barbed wire.
I am trying not to remember
the old house, its glassless windows—

a kitchen knife through a window—
my mother and father in our Kula
house. I don't want to remember,
but the face in this moon
has the same harsh, wiry
gaze. Walls lined with shadows,

bruised fists, for years, I shaded
them with unbroken windows
and fence-posts left unwired,
where our little house in Kula
overlooks all of Maui and the moon
could never ask me to remember.

Once, it was enough to remember
without remembering, to think of shadows
instead of parents, the laughing moon.

I roll up the windows
and park the car. The Kula
wind against my neck. The barbed-wire
fence, glinting silver, running wire
past our house for years. I remember
I was nine when we all left Kula,
my parents spinning shadows
around our secrets—the front window
that perfectly framed the moon—

Crying, my father woke me, the cold moon
in his voice: *Hurry. Now.* And I ran, wiry
from sleep, saw my mother by the window,
pressing a knife to her chest. I remember
her, ashamed and hollow, the shadows
under her eyes. The knife thrown to the Kula

night, the moon as I ran out the door. I remember
falling on barbed-wire, and behind me, two shadows,
boarding up empty windows and mourning our lost Kula.

Tehura

On viewing Gauguin's Mana'o Tupapa'u, The Spirit of the Dead Keep Watch

The chill of violet around you,
Olympia of Oceania, you lie pito down:
a burnished, brown body like mine, draped
over white sheets. And for the moment,
I can't move—How did we get here?
Your framed face turning toward mine,
I see a pleading in your eyes, on your lips

a moan of dread.

Quickly I struck a match, and I saw Tehura,
immobile, naked, lying face downward on the bed:
Feet crossed at the ankle, hands palm down, eyes
inordinately large with fear.

I draw closer to you, mounted on the wall—

Never had I seen her so beautiful, so tremulously beautiful

see waves of dark hair tucked
behind your delicate ear, pulled
violently from your face, neck.
Your seduction rendered—

With a scattering of flowers,
completely naked, waiting for love. Indecent!

through brush strokes of bronze:
arching your back, lifting your chin to meet
a ceaseless stare.

She seemed not to know who I was, and I too
felt a strange uncertainty, in this half-light—

Behind you, the spirit of the dead,

a dangerous apparition only she could see

more his than yours, looms in black, stares—

I was afraid to move. Might she not take me for a tupapa'u?

blankly, unbending. In its hand,
the spark of a bud lights the tiares—

Yet, such coppery beauty, gold skin—

on your mattress, each blossom opening
       into a glorious sneer.

...and the night was soft, soft and ardent, a night of the
tropics...

Tehura, my pōki'i,
in your face I see my own,
the same curves and shadow twisting
into a sad silence. I know
this is not who we are, not Why or How—

only smoke from flailing ghosts, tricks
of fading light, only the wash of gold paint over
       this rotting wood frame.

Note: Italicized stanzas are excerpts from Paul Gauguin's autobio-
graphy, *Noa Noa,* translation by O.F. Theis (1920), selected letters and
journal excerpts.

The Upcountry Drought

Out the screen door to the balcony, the backyard cools
after a day under an obstinate sun. The moonlight casts
its dream glimmer, sifting the color out of trees, grass,
clothes on the line—shadows over silver. Blind orchid
roots cling to the rust-haired stalks of hāpuʻu ferns,
while guava branches bend over beds of impatiens,
like the arms of a mother now able to rest. Yet,
my grandmother lies awake, listening to the quiet thirst
of flowers, interrupted by my grandfather's snores.

A drought has followed her to bed, tonight,
spanning all of upcountry Maui: even the rain
in Haʻikū was not enough. *The plants need water.*
They need shade. They need weeding and pruning.
But the sun swept its heat down in waves today,
an angry ocean, so that they wilted without water.
Their leaves spotted with scorch. And the protea-
They must be watered first—the birds of paradise,
red anthuriums, struggling to lift their flowers, stems,
to unfurl their leaves, so they can be cut, sold wholesale
for only half their worth—*They pay for this house*—
those perfect blooms whose petal tips don't brown,
whose hole-less leaves resist the crawl of thirsty ants.
And the front yard—*It must be watered next*—the hibiscus
bordering the driveway, heliconias and plumerias
by the steps to the lanai—*They must be kept up, too.*
People look at a yard and see the people who own them—
and the grass, the gingers, the gardenias. The sun undoes

the bit of earth in her heat-cracked hands, the water rationed
    for each flower.
Bent by heat, they sleep against the hillside, clinging to their
    helpless soil
like a grandmother's worry to her granddaughter an ocean of
    water away.

Natives Wanted

Do you still hunt and/or gather?
Continue to use plants for healing?
Do you have a dying language
and live in a remote corner
of an island or a rainforest?
Have you contracted foreign diseases
and are now facing cultural extinction?
Do you consistently reject the teachings
of missionaries and settlers?
Do you still chant, sing, and/or dance
as your ancestors did? Do you continue
to revere and/or worship your ancestors?
Do you still wear traditional attire
(i.e. loincloths, feathers, animal skins
or fur, bark cloth, leaves, etc.)
and/or pierce and/or tattoo and/or scar
any part of your body? Have you
maintained your oral traditions
and thus, received sacred knowledge
passed down for at least 5 generations?
Do you now or have you ever
practiced human sacrifice and/or eaten
your enemies (or your friends/family)?
Do you have a long history of burying
priceless treasures with your dead
and still know where they're buried?

If you can answer "yes" to 3 or more of the above
questions, then you are an ideal subject of study
for anthropologists, archaeologists, pharmaceutical
companies, natural historians, museum curators,
colonial writers, missionaries and tourists.

Disclaimer: Compensation for all sacred artifacts and knowledge may
be promised though generally not guaranteed. Side effects of study may
include (but are not limited to): dispossession, displacement, more dis-
ease, chronic colonization, exploitation, diabetes, alcoholism/drug
abuse, severe depression, paranoia, spiritual crisis, and xenophobia.

On Cooking Captain Cook

If you ask the blonde-haired concierge
at the Grand Kīhei, he will tell you
that we ate him whole,
>   strung his white meat on a stick,
>   filled his mouth with apples,
>   and slow-roasted him over fire.

The sunburned vendor selling t-shirts
in Lāhaina will say we ate him, too,
but only certain parts:
>   the head, heart, hands
>   wrapped in a kind of spinach
>   and held over hot lava.

The owner of the Hoola-Hoola Bar
and Grill will say we only ate him
for lack of fine cuisine,
>   rubbed his skin with sea salt
>   then boiled him in coconut milk
>   and served him on a bed of yams.

My anthropology professor, long researching
ancient cultures, will offer explanations
from his latest book:
>   The white-skinned men seemed gods
>   to those without metal or written words.
>   By eating him they meant to become him.

But if you ask my tūtū
while she waters her orchids and protea
she will invite you in
to eat, to eat.

Kalena, 1945

E hāmau o makani mai auaneʻi. *Hush, lest the wind arise.*
—ʻōlelo noʻeau

I was a good daughter, always did like I was told.

Years later, I was rewarded with a house of 5 rooms, an
electric washing machine, and a hapa-haole husband with high
entrepreneurial ambitions, for whom I am a good wife.

For this, my daughter will be rewarded with better beginnings,
speaking perfect ʻŌlelo Pelekane, and learning the haole ways,
which are becoming the only ways, so she may pass.

Then, years from now, as a woman of standing, she will have
enough mana so all this goodness can end.

Papahānaumoku to Hoʻohōkūkalani

E Hoʻohōkūkalani, I sing this song for you,
crafter of stars in the heavens,
would-be bearer of other gods.

E Hoʻohōkūkalani, daughter of land
and sky, sister and mother of Hāloanaka
the still-born, of Hāloa the first to live.

E Hoʻohōkūkalani, buryer of the baby,
curled in the corm-shaped body, mother
and sister of the kalo, which sprung forth.

E Hoʻohōkūkalani, mother of kanaka,
crafter of stars in the heavens,
kuʻu kamaliʻi, I sing this song for you.

Kukui

‘ekahi

You hold within your heart
enough to fire-stir the night,
along with the possibility
of inamona, the sweet roasting
of your meat in communion
with the pa‘akai—a delicate
offering of heat, light and a full ‘ōpū
of properly seasoned poke.

I know you by your gifts.

'elua

Today, I sat under your tangled canopy
of branches and leaned against you,
the shallow ridges of your trunk's bark
against my cheek. Bright bursts
of clouded sky were being reshaped
by your leaves stroking the wind.

Yours is a subtle, unbending hula
timed by the uneven beat of your many
hard-shelled nuts falling against
the grass, and I thought mostly of how easy
it could be to let go of words like that,
to harvest the dark-shelled secrets
that have bent me under their weight.

'ekolu

This should be no secret:
Sometimes there is no justice.
For this is the first time I am writing
that I was molested as a child
by a doctor in his exam room,
where he called it a "physical."

He specialized in asthma, prescribed
pills and steroid inhalers, described
how they would unswell and clear
my esophagus and lungs with the same
clinical precision he used to describe
the soft inside of me as I lay
on the padded table. On the last day
I saw him, I began a thin kind of forgetting.

It took 15 years of struggle
under its weight before I finally told
a counselor, then my family,
then the young policeman
assigned to take my statement—
to give my name, to give
the details, and to patiently repeat
what he couldn't discern in my first telling.

Two weeks later, another policeman
called to tell me that my words
were past the statute of limitations,
but tried to console me with the fact
that my statement would be kept on file.

Yet, I have to believe that there is more
to this life than survival, the expansion

and continuity of breath and flow of blood.
So, sometimes there is no justice,
only the faint ghost of such a thing—

I must let go of this truth, let it fall
to the ground to rot into the soil
where perhaps it can be of some small use.

'ehā

Aloha no e kuʻu kukui ē,
You would have been the Tree of Knowledge
in our Garden of Eden (if we had one).
But it would have taken much more
laborious sinning on Eve's part to eat
your fruit. Rather than just picking you
off the tree, she would have had to forage
on the ground for your round encasement,
just barely breaking open. She would then
have had to peel off the tough brown
outer shell and take your black heart inside
to a big rock, and then find another rock
to kuʻi it open. From there, she would
have to scoop out your nut, then roast it
over a fire before eating it, or suffer
with the runs for a day. It would have taken
much more convincing on the serpent's part,
I think, (if we had one), and Genesis
would have been much, much longer.

But then again, you would have never
been made kapu by any one of our gods,
who, despite their human frailties, were
practical enough to recognize the use
and purpose of knowledge as survival—
fuel for the fire, the clearing of the kai
in an unsettled reef pool, light in the darkness.

And because, as you teach us, there is more
to this life than survival, you offer your nut
to be worn in lei, to be eaten, to heal us
after you have let it go. It is the sweet relish
of all that feeds us in these dark times,
when sometimes there is no justice,
but every day, there is fire and light.

Pele'aihonua

The curl of dawn
meets the leaving night,
lighting the black blanket
of newborn rock, the striations
of red and rainbowed blue
that tātau your skin.
I bring this lei to ask
if I may tread here, to walk
in your house, to ask
for forgiveness. It is not enough,
this circle of lehua and tī
threaded with pule.

Your na'au is churning
in its self-made encasement—
fire-writhing blood
of wahine, ipo, koa, akua—
Pele'aihonua waiting.

Just yesterday I saw a man
stand by an open crevice,
use his hiking stick
to violate you, as if he could
stir your fire and
I thought, if I just pushed him,
slightly, no one would notice.

But he is not the first,
and he is one of many.

I, too, have known
the impulse to destroy,
to obliterate everything
into nothing, my na'au
churning, waiting.

I am not the first—
I, too, am one of many

And as the fires you light
up and down the mountain
remind us, we can harden ourselves
against the salt-pricked wind.

Akā, inā kulaʻi wau, e huki ʻoe, e kuʻu akua ē?

Papatuanuku

E hoʻolohe ʻoukou e nā mamo o Hāloa—

Remember who you came from,
the first hā I gave you, binding you
to me. It is my blood coursing
through you, the lush fruit of my body
feeding you, my ʻili stretched beneath
you, its redness from which you
were formed, and my voice you hear
as your children call for you in the night,
hungry and tired with nowhere to go.

Go to them now. Hear them and hear me:

Flags hoisted, may be lowered,
spears thrown, cannons, guns,
and nuclear bombs fired, treaties
and constitutions, palapala bound
and broken. Nations rise and fall
with the tides, and your boundaries
of pepa might as well be written
in dust, for empires burn to ashes
in a fire of their own making
and will only be forgotten in the end,
when only I will remain. And through me,
so will you. He ʻoia mau no kākou.

IV. Hāloa Naka

The Kula House

It can be horrible
what a house can hold
onto, even long after
the living have moved
on. You see it in the pine
board knots that look
like eyes back toward
the koa and eucalyptus,
beyond the broken
barbed-wire fence
where the fog sits, waiting.

They've seen that a house
can be rebuilt with new
wood and some varnish,
the mold bleached over,
all the glass cleared
of webs and the remnants
of the last few upcountry rains—

but it needs much more
to clean itself of memory.

Ka ʻŌlelo

O ke alelo ka hoe uli o ka ʻōlelo a ka waha. *The tongue is the steering paddle of the words uttered by the mouth.*—ʻōlelo noʻeau

ʻekahi

Think of all the lost words, still unspoken,
waiting to be given use again, claimed,
or for newly born words to unburden
them of their meanings. There are winds and rains
who have lost their names, descending the slopes
of every mountain, each lush valley's mouth,
and the songs of birds and moʻo, that cope
with our years of slow unknowing, somehow.
It was not long ago that ʻōlelo
was silenced, along with its *dying race,*
who lived, then thrived, reverting to the old
knowing words. English could never replace
the land's unfolding song, nor the ocean's
ancient oli, giving us use again.

'elua

Like the sea urchin leaves, pimpling its shell
as its many spines let go, turn to sand,
my great-grandfather's Hawaiian words fell
silent, while his children grew, their skin tanned
and too thin to withstand the teacher's stick,
reprimands demanding English only.
The law lasted until 1986,
after three generations of family
swallowed our 'ōlelo like pōhaku,
learned to live with the cold, dark fruit under
our tongues. This is our legacy—words strewn
among wana spines in the long record
the sand has kept within its grains, closer
to reclaiming our shells, now grown thicker.

'ekolu

Ka 'ōlelo has a lilting rhythm
arising from the coastal mountains' moans
as they loosen their salted earth, succumb
to the ocean and its hunger for stone.
It carries the cadence of nā waihī,
born from the fresh rain in nā waipuna
and flowing past the fruiting 'ulu trees,
wiliwili, kukui, and koa.
It holds the song my grandfather longs for
most, as he remembers his father's voice,
and regrets not asking him to speak more
Hawaiian, so that he may have the choice
to offer words in his inheritance,
knowing his 'ohā will not be silenced.

'ehā

Think of all the old words that have succumbed,
their kaona thrown oceanward for English
words we use like nets to catch the full sum
of our being, finding too little fish
caught in the mesh, even as we adjust
the gauge, reshaping them to suit our mouths.
I must admit I love the brittle crust
my untrained tongue's foreignness forms; it crowns
the dark, churning pith of prenatal earth
rising in the volcano's throat, unspoken
for now, founding my wide island of words.
And kaona, a ho'okele's current,
circles during my wa'a's slow turn inward,
steering my tongue through each old word learned.

'elima

As the 'ape shoot, whose delicate shoots
shoot forth their young sprouts, and spread, and bring forth
in their birth, many branches find their roots
in the dark, wet 'ōlelo the earth bore.
My unripe tongue taps my palate, my teeth,
like a blind ko'e that must feel its way
through the liquids, mutes and aspirates of speech,
the threading of breath and blood into lei:
"E aloha. 'O wai kou inoa?"
I ask, after the language CD's voice.
"'O Kekauoha ko'u inoa,"
my grandfather answers, "Pehea 'oe?"
So, we slowly begin, with what 'ōlelo
we know; E ho'oulu ana kākou.

Hāloanaka

There is no need to sweeten
    your body's ripe offering
to suit my open mouth.

        I take you in, as you are—
    the taste of earth and light,
            salt-wind sieved through valley rains.

           Just days ago, your heart-
               shaped leaves faced the sun,
           funneling light and warmth

              through your long trembling
                  stalks. You felt the soft earth
              open itself to your roots,

          whose blind strands fed
              the crystalline nebulae
          that once purpled your corm.

Still, you give yourself over
and over again, e hiapo,

your sacrifice made ripe
in the soil's short incubation—

so that we may live knowing love
and ʻohana, our bright belonging.

On a Routing Slip from the U.S. Postal Service, Pukalani Branch

Received 7 April 2002, after careful inspection in New Zealand

16 March 2002
Brandy,

This poi was frozen—hopefully
it'll keep until it gets to you.

You'll need to microwave it
(like how I told you—with water).

Hope it's not too sour. Maybe
I'll send the fresh poi next time.

Love you,
Grandpa

Long Distance

I admit there are times it seems easier this way.
I wake up softly with the sun every morning,

without any black-out lining on the curtains.
I make myself coffee and a bowl of sugar-cereal,

instead of the muesli you insist on. The dishes
are left in the sink all day while I'm at work,

sometimes staying later than I told you I would,
and I feel absolutely no guilt. When I do return

home, I eat whatever my animal stomach craves—
pieces of fruit with peanut butter spooned straight

from the jar, milk drunk from the carton, some poke
and poi, if there's any left from the night before.

Then I watch crime and home-improvement shows,
even "Charmed" re-runs, and there are no negotiations.

In fact, I could stay up all night, with all the lights,
stereo, *and* t.v. on, painting the living room purple—

and nothing. And it would be perfect, too, if only
I could sleep through the night despite feeling

the weight of your absence on the left side of the bed.

Synaptic Collisions

I take the poem as it comes, a catalogue
of fragments declaring itself *yours*—

A verdant asthenosphere spurred by dream,
in my electric net of synaptic

collisions. It calls the bright wild of you
beneath the night's star-river communion,

the moon's slow, deliberate decrescendo
behind the blue hills—the full weight of you

falling into me. I have memorized
the soft forest in your eyes, the sweet, dark

air under those trees, where I planned the path
my lips should take next, my fingers tracing

the lines of your palms. For now, it's enough
to hold the blooming sky of those mornings

still beside you in my celluloid mind—
I have a poet's memory for such things

and a love for you, constant as the rise
and recession of the tides, the slow climb

of new islands toward the ocean's surface,
patient as this Pacific between us.

September Wedding, Afternoon Light

'ekahi

There's a photograph of you I took with me:
your hair's cut short, a dark vermillion shade

strewn with sun-glitter like those fiber-optic
wands at next month's county fair. You wear

a white wife-beater and clipped, vamp nails;
your hands are white orchids in the wind.

You watch yourself in the side mirror,
blue eyes over the rim of your movie-star

sunglasses, while I drive us somewhere,
though nowhere we haven't been; a lei

of rainbow silk flowers swings between us
from the rear-view—at its center, the road.

'elua

I prefer to drive to your childhood house
at night with only the light of a full moon.

Windows down, I pass the silvered pastures,
the shadow of Mule Hill we climbed to see

Maui, city-lit, the blue flashes of Kahului
Airport guiding the last planes in; I take it

all in: flowering jacaranda, lantana, scrolls
of eucalyptus bark peeling from the trunk.

Tonight, I'll drive away from your house
on the same road, hoping for the same moon.

'ekolu

Pages of images of us, half-faced and out
of focus, our cheeks curved into crescent

moons closing our eyes. We're often animals
of night, eclipsed, caught frozen in that flash

of light. Over and over we pick the dream-fruit
whose flesh is ripe, the heart open for carving.

You would say, even then, all you wanted
was a small wedding, on Maui, so it could be

with all those you love: a flood of island
flowers in bloom, the Pacific Ocean in view.

'ehā

Your groom is the only one to survive
our private island of girlhood, the mud

pool we swim in after months spent apart:
He hands you the phone and closes the door

with careful hands. Once, I watched him hold
your rose stems underwater, trimming each

before easing them into your kitchen vase.
Despite this, the light on the water's surface

barely rippled. *They will last longer this way,*
he assured me, and I still don't doubt him.

'elima

Not many men could live in a trailer for love,
then fly to an island, lush as it is, to marry.

You know this, trust his hands as they hold
yours like orchids, and love him, love you.

For your wedding, let there be a haku lei
of clouds for Haleakalā behind you both,

the wind's hula through the king protea
at your sides, and a blessing of light rain

above you—the afternoon sky come alive
in your eyes, sunlight caught, enraptured.

Ode to the Couch We Reupholstered

Granted, we never claimed to be professionals.
There are enough staples throughout the wood
frame's seams to officially turn it metal, the white
corduroy we used, improper for upholstery, gathers
lint in its ridges and has already lost its tautness.
Still, I fell asleep on it after you left this morning,

knowing we made it much better than it was—
the dirt-ridden pinstripe and lumpy pillows
would have been snubbed by even the night's
furniture scavengers, and after them, only
a dump's incineration was certain for a couch,
mass-assembled at birth with so much promise.

It has new life now, and a sense of belonging
in our modest apartment of things left behind
but given use—of wood veneered tables, misshapen
lamps missing their shades, of unseen dust traps
like family we learn to live with. I know it's true
that made things are infused with our own spirits

before we lay our hands upon them, perhaps even
before thoughts of their creation enter our minds—
but I wonder if this couch's spirit entered me, as well?
I feel I belong here, too, on this couch, beside you,
planning to make and remake more with you, to always
look upon a thing, and see its glorious possibility.

The Dream of Kahāʻula

Hāpai, Lehua wakes in a dream of red
pouring like lava to the floor where red
wraps her ankles in red ripples like blood
blooming from broken skin, over red
pictures of a young Nani, a lei crowning
her long, dark hair, through the dim-lit red
kitchen, between dried aku and a bowl of red
chili shoyu, to each wall, every corner—red
climbing up Lehua's knees, waist, chest, mouth, red
rolling earth, burying her and raising red

        in the the old Hāʻiku house,
            now full with the red breath of life, *Kahāʻula.*

Years later, Kahāʻula asked how his name happened—
And what did it mean?—and no one could answer.
His mother died with the secret, giving life to her only son.
In a dream—his father told him—Your name
was shown to her before you were born. *But why?*
Kahāʻula cried, so Grandma Nani told him more
of the fringed flower his mother was named for,
how they bloom like blood through broken skin,
burn red on the barest of branches, rise even
through lava rock and ash, how the wind whispers
red to the highest blossom on the tallest tree—

And of *her* dream, of Lehua, before her daughter was born,
        of red lehua fringes floating like lit matches on the water.

Tūtū, Speaking of the Rain

I was told once a long time ago that I looked beautiful
in the rain and I must say, Lani-girl, it was true.

My tutu stood on the porch, calling me: *Puni!*
Hele mai, you hard-headed girl. You'll catch cold.
Hele mai and dry that hair of yours, 'auē!

'Ae, I was kolohe, pretending not to hear her voice,
carried by the wind. But not out of disrespect, Lani—
We had an understanding, the rain and I,

to meet everyday by Hina's silver pools
of moonlight swallowed deep in Hāna.
My arms spread wide as Wākea, I never waited long.

Ua always came, sweeping through my hair,
streaming over my body's curves until his mana
collapsed into a puddle, a halo at my feet.

Oh, Lani-girl, how could I come in from the rain after that?

Hōʻailona

There are secrets the rain should not speak of.
There are whispers in each drop of water born
from smaller drops, spun finely into clouds, older
than the mountains. But it speaks to me at night,
when no one is awake, but me, inside a dream.

In that dream there is a window which stays shut
so the water can tap against the glass and tell me
its story. It needs to tell someone, it tells me.
Even something as old and strong, cannot hold
all the words. They need to get out, out past
the dams, over bridges and umbrellas, beyond
the molecular bonds of hydrogen and oxygen.

I can listen for now, I tell it, *tell me,* and so
it begins, tapping how there once was an eel
or a word that came out of the ocean, out
of a mouth. The mouth was wide open.
It yawned for ten billion years, as the night yawns,
as a leaf yawns, unfurling. It could not speak
its name. But it knew. It knew. Its name
was a word like an eel, a slippery eel, like a word
from a mouth like the sea, like a yawn. Dark blue.
Eyes blinking with the waves, it waited. Waves
through water, across water, called from water
to water. The rise and fall of dark blue waves
blinking and quiet, quiet, calm to nothing. Alone.

Like that, the rain returns to itself in its story—
words fall in circles, repeat, then turn. Rain
taps the names of each secret, whipping its tongue
like a slippery eel against my dream's window.
I hope it never suspects I don't understand;
I need to hear how it ends—
                              Wait. There it is again. Listen.

Lei Niho Palaoa

You have lived through decades under glass,
a velvet bust replacing the one
you once held with love. A thousand strands
of our people's hair were given
to plait your chains; a palaoa offered
a tusk for your hook-shaped pendant.

Your crafters chanted prayers as they worked:
measuring each hair, blending each end
into a new braid, searching the bone
for fractures, carving the inverted arc
of your hook. The days they spent show
the generations of knowing your art.

So, sit proudly in your museum room.
Your people will come for you soon.

He Mele Aloha no Albert Wendt
a me Reina Whaitiri

me ka mahalo nui loa

Everywhere are the ihe
    you've helped to carve
        from the whispering kauila,
            the barbs hewn

by the eager hands that hurl them—
    the same that anticipate their return,
    and catch them mid-flight.

There are the hulu
    you've woven alongside us
        into the 'ahu
            of the Ko'olau's folds,
                the makana of kalo,
            niu, 'uala, 'ulu, mai'a, and i'a
    this 'āina has fed you, too,

and the 'ili 'ili birthing themselves
    in the na'au of Papa
    bathed by the rain of Wākea—
        they've shown you
            how they make themselves
                        mountains.

And everywhere, we are beginning to hear
    our voices rising with yours
        like a pahu
        invoking Manaiakalani
            from the writhing depths of Pōuliuli,
        while the wa'a of Māui
            is unearthed and ready

    to guide us over the waves.

Over and Over the Return, Moʻokūʻauhau

There is so much in the wind's warm engulfment
as it makes its way from the green-robed mauna,
combing the tī stalks, palms, kukui, and pines
toward Hanalei Bay, where the water rolls itself

into long, untied strands of white salted lei,
as it meets the sand over and over.

Using the map my grandfather drew of the town
he left 66 years ago, I found his older brother,
an uncle I never knew, whose life ended at thirteen
in the piko of Hanalei Bay, the undertow pulling him

down into the ocean's throat before also
swallowing the man who tried to save him.

I cleared his shaded grave of dried lauhala and graying niu
and returned the fallen chain-post to its cracked, concrete
hole.
My grandfather will be happy to hear of the red
and green tī, a keiki growing wild at his feet,

for when the Kekauoha's left for Lāʻie, this brother
was the only one left behind, in the only home he ever knew,
cradled by nā mauna at his head and at his feet.

Soon, the wind will carry its delicate fragrance
of commingled pine needles, old kukui shells and niu husk,
all the salt of its journey, infinitesimal pieces of broken bottles
under the naupaka, and everything else unseen and nearly
    forgotten

turned to sand. This same wind will return
to the same folds of mauna, offering over and over
its gifts, and like nā kūpuna, always leaving, always returning.

Waiting for the Sunrise at Haleakalā

Still half-asleep, I drive toward the summit
and find a rhythm turning sharp corners,
leaning with each familiar curve. Outside,
the dark forms of abandoned 'ahu,
built by some ancestral hand, and high crowns
of silversword stand solemnly in black.
Above them, stars dim, slow as the rented
cars ahead, an uneasy Hertz convoy.
I curse them silently, knowing this road
and the view down of Maui, the muted
flickering of an island city's lights—
what distracts the rustle of tourist maps.
The fog filters our headlights, as our cars,
imposing on the calm, find their spaces.
In the unlit cold, a voiceless wind waits
for our doors to open, heaters to stop.
I carry blankets up the gazer trail
to the crater's edge and sit, staring down
a mouth full of blue clouds, a restless tide
covering, then clearing over the black.

Sitting here, above the clouds, I wonder
why I came, what led me to this sacred
place, expecting that it could awaken
the lost beginnings of my blood—answer
my dream of lava touching ocean, belts of steam
blown by the wind, green shoots of fern through rock.
Waking from this dream tonight, cold, restless,
afraid of forgetting where I came from,
I knew only to climb higher, to reach
the summit before sunrise, as Maui-
a-ka-malo did long ago. Lying here
against the cinder, he waited to snare
the sun, its sixteen hurried rays, with reins
of olonā. And I feel the same need
to slow the days, in their constant sway
of golf courses over graves and hotels
over heiau. Each hour soars as quick

as the jets above this child-shaped island
lost in traffic on the highways, the wind-
driven canefields burnt long into the night—
from Pukalani to Kīhei, Kula
to Lāhaina—no rest for paradise.

I close my eyes to listen to the air,
hoping to hear the ancient chants of hā
upwelling from the valleys, the still breath
of life, the inviolate sigh of love
I know lives in iwi beneath me, in rocks
born in the crater, lying where they fell.
But I hear nothing in the wind and clouds,
as the sky turns from black to blue, singing
a silent aubade to the swallowed stars,
to Maui, fading slowly with the moon.
Then, as the sun begins to stretch its rays,
lighting my tears, I remember how words
cannot hold such love flooding the valleys,
the aloha in pink roselani
buds blooming wild, full of new mountain rain.

Below, the clouds thin, and the crater floor
awakens, enrobed in red and gold cinder,
flush of color woven into the earth.
And the tourists applaud the performance
before walking to their cars, turning back
for one last look at the sun in its house,
another camera's bright flash. But I stay,
easing off the blanket from my shoulders,
under a sun so close, I could touch it.
And I am grateful for the quiet lull,
for the time to sit among the scattered
grass, the silversword reaching for the sky—
and one lets me watch, opening its fire
in five hundred red flowers, each a sun
offering light from Haleakalā.

About the Author

 From Upcountry Maui, Brandy Nālani McDougall is of Kanaka Maoli, Chinese and Scottish ancestry. She is a Kamehameha Schools graduate who completed her M.F.A. in Poetry from the University of Oregon in 2001 and a Fulbright Study Award (Aotearoa/New Zealand) in 2002. An award-winning poet, she has been published in journals and anthologies throughout Hawai'i, the continental U.S. and the Pacific. She is an Associate Editor for Kuleana 'Ōiwi Press, the publisher of *'ōiwi: a native hawaiian journal,* whose mission is to publish, promote, and support Kanaka Maoli literature, arts, and literacy. She is also the cofounder of a student-run press called Kahuaomānoa, which is dedicated to publishing individual collections of student art and literature. In 2006, she received the Grace K.J. Abernethy Fellowship in publishing from the international journal *Mānoa,* where she is now an Associate Editor. She is currently pursuing a Ph.D. in English, focusing on contemporary Kanaka Maoli Literature, from the University of Hawai'i at Mānoa. This is her first collection of poetry.

Mahalo to the editors of the following publications in which these poems first appeared:

Whetu Moana: "Emma, 1993," "Salt-Wind of Waihe'e," "Ma'alaea Harbor, Father's Day," "Petroglyphs at Olowalu," "Lei Niho Palaoa" and "Dirty Laundry"

'ōiwi: a native hawaiian journal: "Red Hibiscus in the Rain" and "Cane Spider"

Hawai'i Pacific Review: "Tūtū, Speaking of the Rain" and "Waiting for the Sunrise at Haleakalā"

Bamboo Ridge: "How I Learned to Write My Name" and "On Finding My Father's First Essay"

Trout: "Back When We Lived With Ghosts" and "Koa and the Burning of the Kula House"

Tinfish: "Haumea"

Ahani: Indigenous American Poetry: "Hāloa Naka," "The History of this Place," and "Pō"

Mantis: "Dream of Kahā'ula"

Honolulu Weekly: "Koa and the Burning of the Kula House"

Ka Wai Ola o OHA: "Ka 'Ōlelo"

Indigenous Encounters: Exploring Relations Between People in the Pacific: "Huaka'i"

CPSIA information can be obtained at www.ICGtesting.com
Printed in the USA
BVOW022247221112

306209BV00005B/58/P